North York Moors

Compiled by
Dennis and Jan Kelsall

TRAVEL

JARROLD
publishing

Mapping sourced from **OS** Ordnance Survey

Acknowledgements

The authors wish to express their thanks to the staff of the North York Moors National Park and English Nature for their kind help.

Text: Dennis and Jan Kelsall
Photography: Dennis and Jan Kelsall
Editor: Crawford Gillan
Designer: Doug Whitworth

Jarrold Publishing ISBN 0-7117-2428-8

First published 2003
by Jarrold Publishing

Printed in Belgium
by Proost NV, Turnhout. 1/03

...old Publishing
...hfinder Guides, Whitefriars,
...wich NR3 1TR
...ail: pathfinder@jarrold.com
...v.jarrold-publishing.co.uk

...nt cover: Bilsdale
...vious page: Sheep graze the lush ...er slopes of Bilsdale

AB		MM	
MA		MN	
MB		MO	
MC		MR	
MD		MT	
ME	5 03	MW	
MG			
MH			

Contents

Keymap

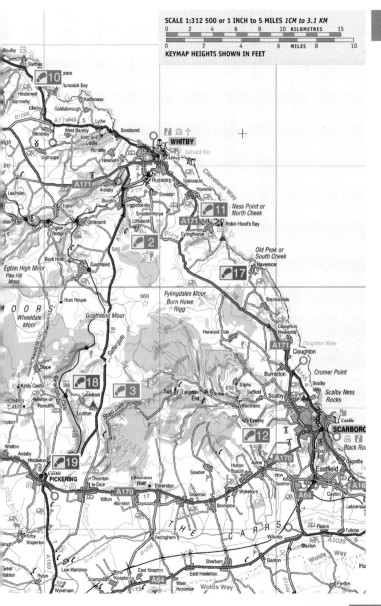

Boulby
Staithes
grave
Runswick Bay
Hinderwell
Ellerby
Borrowby
Kettleness
Goldsborough
B1266
A174645 5 Lythe
Mickleby
West Barnby
Sandsend
Multrave
Castle
Dunsley
Newholm
Ugthorpe
WHITBY
Saltwick Bay
Abbey
Leaholm
A171
Aislaby
Ruswarp
Stainsacre
Sneaton
Hawsker
Egton
Sleights
Uggelarnby
Grosmont
Sneatonthorpe
Littlebeck

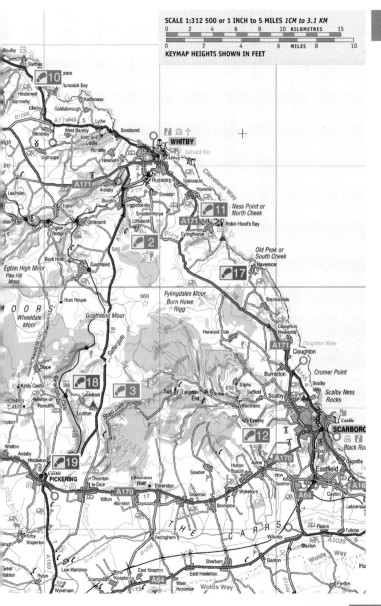

Ness Point or
North Cheek
Robin Hood's Bay

Beck Hole
Goathland
Fylingthorpe

Old Peak or
South Cheek
Ravenscar

Egton High Moor
Pike Hill
Moss

Hunt House
959
Fylingdales Moor
Burn Howe
Rigg

Staindale
O O R S
Wheeldale
Moor
Goathland Moor
18
Harwood Dale
Cloughton
Newlands
Cloughton Wyke
A171
Cloughton

Stape
Keldy Castle
18
Levisham
Newton on
Rawcliffe
3
Toll
Langdale
End
Broxa
656
Silpho
Suffield
Scalby
Mills
Burniston
Cromer Point
Scalby
Scalby Ness
Rocks
Hackness

ROMAN
CAMP
Lockton

ropton
Wrelton
Aislaby
Middleton
19
Castle
PICKERING
Thornton-
le-Dale
Wilton
Allerston
Ebberston
Hall
Ebberston
A170
17
Snainton
Wykeham
Brompton
Everley
12
Hutton
Buscel
Ayton
A170
Irton
Seamer
A64
SCARBORO
Castle
Black Ro
Osgodby
Eastfield
A16
Cayton

Kirby
Misperton
Yedingham
T H E
C A R R S
Willerby
River Hertford
Flixton
Folkton
A1039
6

Great
Habion
Ryton
Low Marishes
West
Knapton
East Knapton
Sherburn
Ganton
Wolds
Way
Staxton
B1249
Hu

Wykeham
Scampston
East
Knapton
A64
East Heslerton
West
Heslerton
Wolds Way
Fordon

Introduction

The North York Moors are deservedly recognised as one of the most beautiful regions of England, but 'moor' is hardly sufficient to describe the diversity of landscapes and multiplicity of appeal that exist within its bounds. Seen in the vague half-light of a wet and windy winter's afternoon, the earlier name of Blackamore – 'black hill moor' – is perhaps a fitting description for the awesome vastness of its rolling upland, where hardly anything, be it the work of nature or man, interrupts the long skyline. Yet witness it again, illuminated by a shaft of sunlight stabbing through low, scudding clouds, or clad in regal splendour by the flowering ling, and you will realise that it is a place of endless change, where each passing hour brings a subtle variation of mood.

Dales, woods and sea

Wander into the dales and you will discover a different world, where sparkling streams cascade over rocky beds and tree-fringed rivers snake across lush grass meadows. Idyllic villages and picturesque farmsteads nestle within their folds, surrounded by orderly fields that probe the limits of viable cultivation. In some places the land is silvan, but not all is commercial forest, for there remain many places where native species prevail, harking back to the wild woodland that once covered much of the country. And, in the east, rugged cliffs, sheltered coves and sweeping sands draw an erratic boundary between the opposing elements of land and sea. Everywhere has its own character and charm, and invites a leisurely exploration and contemplation.

Human enterprise

Yet this wild and beautiful landscape is not necessarily all that it appears, for the hand of man has played a far greater role in shaping the countryside than you might at first think. Throughout, the high moors bear evidence of prehistoric settlement, in scattered burial mounds, territorial boundary dykes and agricultural enclosures; traces of the first farmers who tamed the primeval uplands. Early medieval monks also left their mark, not only in the evocative ruins of the vast monastic houses raised in isolated valleys, but by managing the uplands as immense sheep walks. They organised mining for iron and coal, enterprises, which, during the Industrial Revolution, turned some of the remotest settlements into boom towns almost overnight. Quarrying for stone, alum and other minerals changed the face of the moors and a considerable network of tramways and railways rapidly reached out to service them. The coast, too, was alive with

Repairing stone walls requires an expert hand

activity; the few safe landings along its rocky and dangerous shores were among the most productive fishing villages on the English eastern seaboard and Whitby grew to be a major trading port and whaling station. For better or worse, those days and their industry have passed, and a new balance between man's activities and nature prevails. The legacy is a land still rich in natural beauty, enhanced by the relics left behind by the trail of human toil and endeavour.

A place to walk

Sparsely populated and with relatively few roads, the Moors are best explored on foot, and there are some 1,400 miles of designated rights-of-way as well as many other paths and tracks along which it is permissible to walk. Some of these date from the monastic era and were, in effect, the

Boarding the train for Newtondale at Grosmont

motorways of their day, connecting the monasteries with their outlying granges and the markets to which produce was taken. As you roam across the open moors, you will come across stone-flagged paths and isolated standing stones, crosses and markers, set up in antiquity to guide travellers safely across the otherwise featureless expanse. One of the best-known is Young Ralph's Cross at the head of Rosedale, which has been adopted as the emblem of the North York Moors National Park. Encompassing some 544 square miles (1,436 km²) and the third most visited of the country's national parks, it is perhaps a fitting coincidence that this book is published in the year during which it celebrates its golden jubilee.

Discover the countryside

With so many pathways and different places to visit, the difficulty is not finding somewhere to go, but rather deciding just where to begin. A good place, particularly if you are new to the area, is one of the two National Park centres, to be found at Danby and Sutton Bank. Fascinating displays and exhibitions offer an ideal introduction, and the short walks from each illustrate disparate aspects of the moor, demonstrating its capacity for beauty and surprise. Other walks in this collection reveal some of the Moor's most outstanding natural features; the dramatic Hole of Horcum, the enigmatic rocks at Bridestones and the splendid tumbling waters of Falling Foss. As well as exploring the high moors, where the strange calling of the grouse is never far away, wander through verdant dales such as the beautiful Farndale, whose Lenten lilies carpet the riverside meadows in celebration of spring's arrival. In contrast are areas that were exploited by industry, such as the coastal cliffs at Ravenscar, excavated for their alum-bearing shale, or the now peaceful village and valley of Rosedale, once filled with 'work hard, play hard' miners who dug into the hillside for its rich iron ore.

Other places to visit

Follow these walks to discover some fascinating ancient buildings; the atmospheric ruins of the great abbey communities at Rievaulx and Byland or the stark, defensive, medieval stone piles of Pickering and Helmsley. Very different is the magnificently restored Duncombe Park and, at Nunnington, there is another splendid country house to visit. The small market towns and picturesque villages, from which many of the routes begin, also have much of interest and are worthy of exploration, particularly their churches, often the oldest building standing. Other walks pass fine museums, while at Spout House you will find a wonderfully preserved country inn, and if you fancy a ride on a steam train, there is even one ramble that utilises the North York Moors Railway. Above all, this collection of walks is about enjoyment, and in each one, short or long, you will find that there is much to delight.

The Pepper Pot

1 *Danby Lodge to Clitherbeck*

START Danby Lodge Moors Centre

DISTANCE 2½ miles (4km)

TIME 1½ hours

PARKING Car park opposite Danby Lodge (pay and display)

ROUTE FEATURES Moorland and field paths, moderate climb at the start

If you have not visited the North York Moors before, the Moors Centre is an ideal place to begin your exploration, where exhibitions explain the area's history and its influence on the countryside we enjoy today. Discover something of the vast emptiness of the open moor and the seclusion of its sheltered valleys, two contrasting features of a wonderful landscape.

From the road junction by the Moors Centre, a waymarked path climbs through a beech wood, and on at the edge of pasture above. Turn through the second gate, 150 yds (137m) along and strike diagonally across to continue up beside the wall. At the top, bear right around the corner to reach a crossing track at the edge of the moor.

Ⓐ Turn right, but a few paces along, at a junction in front of a gate, go left. A broad track briefly rises over a crest before undulating

The moors around **Danby** were not always desolate and featureless, and there is ample evidence to show that 3,000 years ago, during the Bronze Age, it supported a relatively large population. Numerous barrows, field enclosures and settlement sites have been identified on the riggs above the deep valleys, as well as a 5-ft (2-m) high monolith, once part of a 42-ft (13-m) diameter stone circle.

across the immense openness of the moor. Some 300 years ago, this lonely upland was mined for its coal, which lies in shallow seams just below the surface, and

PUBLIC TRANSPORT Irregular bus service past Danby Lodge, rail and bus service to Danby (1 mile)

REFRESHMENTS Tea room and picnic area at Moors Centre

PUBLIC TOILETS At Moors Centre

ORDNANCE SURVEY MAPS Explorer OL27 (North York Moors – Eastern Area)

CHILDRENS PLAY AREA At Moors Centre

evidence of that activity is revealed in the heather-covered hollows and mounds that lie beside the path. After almost ¾ mile (1.2km), the track ends at a road.

B Walk right along it to cross to cross Black Beck and then turn off through a gate on the right to follow the edge of the field away from the road. Keep going in the next field to enter the yard at

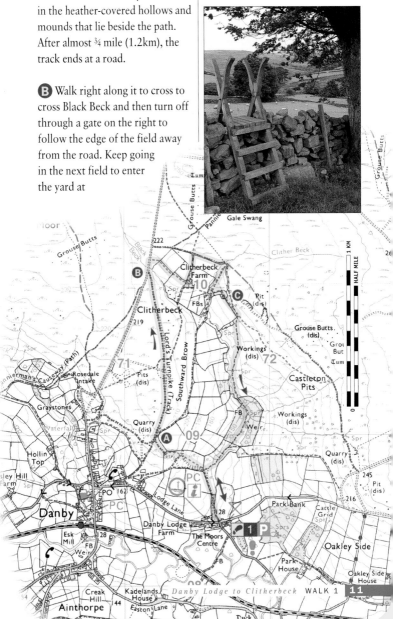

The stile beside Clitherbeck Farm

Along the Dale above Clitherbeck

Clitherbeck Farm then leave along a track, immediately on the left. It shortly leads to a junction, where, to the right, a bridle path descends to a bend and crosses Clither Beck. Look for a stile on the right, over which, follow the stream down for some 250 yds (239m) to meet a wall and then turn left, climbing away beside it.

Originally a simple farmhouse overlooking the River Esk, **Danby Lodge** was extended in the 19th century into a comfortable shooting lodge. It has been the National Park Information Centre since 1976.

C Turn through a gate, a little way up, and walk on, passing the ruin of a tiny farmstead to another gate just beyond it. Back on the edge of open moor, keep ahead, initially being guided by a wall. Carry on beyond its end, now on a clear path that falls gently along the valley side. At the bottom, continue downstream, shortly crossing a wall stile to reach a footbridge. Once over, go left to a gate and on across an open meadow below a bank, planted with saplings. More gates take the way ahead, rising through the plantation before climbing across open grazing to join a wall at the top. Walk left, now retracing your way back to Danby Lodge. ●

Across a stream behind the car park is a delightful wood, what bird is it named after?

Falling Foss

2

START Forest car park, south of Littlebeck
DISTANCE 1½ miles (2.4km)
TIME 1½ hours
PARKING Car park at start of walk
ROUTE FEATURES Woodland paths with some moderate ascents

Approaching the end of their 178-mile (300km) trek, 'Coast to Coast' walkers often tarry in Littlebeck's enchanting, ravine-like valley before bracing muscle and sinew for the final stage to the North Sea. This ramble past Falling Foss and a curious woodland shelter gives a taste of the sights encountered along the way, and might inspire you to tackle that worthy pilgrimage.

🥾 Opposite the entrance to the car park, a woodland path leaves through a gap beside the main track, dropping into the valley. Shortly, where it levels to a junction by a broken stone wall, go sharp left onto a narrow path. Clinging to the almost sheer, valley

The path to Falling Foss

After heavy rain, **Falling Foss** is a tremendous spectacle, as May Beck plunges over a 50-ft (15-m) ledge in a torrent of spray and white foam. The cottage beside it, **Midge Hall**, was built by Sir James Wilson for his gamekeeper, and more lately housed a small museum. Sadly it is now becoming derelict.

PUBLIC TRANSPORT None
REFRESHMENTS Picnic tables by car park
PUBLIC TOILETS None
ORDNANCE SURVEY MAPS Explorer OL27 (North York Moors – Eastern Area)

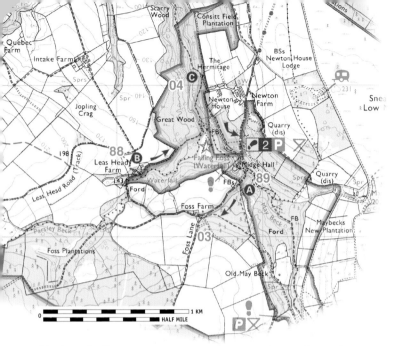

side, the path offers a dramatic view through the trees to the beck far below, before descending easily towards the head of Falling Foss and a small forest cottage, blessed with the rather grandiose title 'Midge Hall'.

A Cross the footbridge beyond the cottage and climb to the main track above. Turn right and follow it uphill, shortly leaving the trees to reach the barns of Foss Farm. Keep to the main track, bearing right in front of the buildings and walk on for another 300 yds (274m) to a waymark. A bridleway is signed off to the right, which follows the perimeter of a couple of fields, descending to a gate in the far corner at the edge of a wood. Across a bridge, the way bends right to Leas Head Farm. Just before reaching the buildings,

> Cut from solid sandstone and entered by an impressive Gothic doorway, **The Hermitage's** roomy circular chamber, around which runs a surprisingly comfortable (at least after a long day's walking) stone bench, provides an ideal lunchtime shelter on a rainy day. And when the sun shines, you can perch on the belvedere outside to enjoy the view. The initials above the entrance are of George Chubb, who was schoolmaster in the nearby village.

go left over a stile and then follow the boundary wall right, passing the front of the cottage and its attendant buildings.

B Pass through a gap in the wall at the far end and walk beside a barn and over a stile into a small paddock. Bear right behind the buildings to another stile into Great Wood. After an initial drop, the way then wanders gently downhill through the trees above a deep valley, eventually descending to meet the stream running at its base. Walk on to cross a couple of footbridges, beyond which the path continues ahead, rising determinedly above Little Beck. Before long, the way suddenly levels at a junction of paths by The Hermitage.

C To the left, the path continues through the valley, emerging at Littlebeck, ¾ mile (1.2km) away. It makes an excellent extension to the walk and leads past another small waterfall, but unfortunately, there is neither pub nor café in the hamlet. The way back, however, lies to the right. At a fork, a little way along, bear right, but then, when you reach a second junction, go left, returning along your outward passage to the car park. ●

> **?** *When was The Hermitage cut from its boulder?*

The Hermitage

3 *The Bridestones*

START Low Staindale off Dalby Forest Drive (toll road)
DISTANCE 1½ miles (2.4km)
TIME 1½ hours
PARKING Car park at start of walk
ROUTE FEATURES Clear paths throughout, but with a moderate climb onto the moor

Although any number of pathways and tracks penetrate Dalby Forest, this short walk is as spectacular as any you might choose. It leads through a delightful valley before rising onto the moor above, where curious outcroping rocks, the Bridestones, have been carved into weird and wonderful shapes by the wind, rain and frost.

A path leads west from the back of the car park across an open meadow towards trees. Spanning a stream, a bridge takes the way on through a kissing gate into the Bridestones nature reserve. Ignore a path to the right and walk ahead along the valley at the edge of a wood shortly reaching a beck crossed by a ford.

A However, stay on this bank and turn upstream through a gate into Dove Dale. Over a bridge, continue by the beck, later re-crossing higher up at the mouth of Bridestones Griff. The path carries on ahead, steadily climbing a well-made path that rises along the ridge separating the two valleys. As you gain height, pause to look out across the valley, when some of the Bridestones come into view on the

There are two groups of these strangely weathered rocks that break the emptiness of the open moor, known as **High and Low Bridestones** respectively. Composed of sandstone laid down during the Jurassic period some 150 million years ago, alternating bands of relative hardness have led to their uneven erosion, producing the odd shapes we see today.

PUBLIC TRANSPORT Seasonal bus service through Dalby Forest
REFRESHMENTS Picnic tables by car park, refreshments at Low Dalby Visitor Centre (3 miles)
PUBLIC TOILETS By car park
ORDNANCE SURVEY MAPS Explorer OL27 (North York Moors – Eastern Area)

High Bridestones

skyline. Levelling at the top, the way continues easily over heather heath, leading you to the first of the fantastic formations.

B Where the track then splits, go right, dipping across the head of the valley over the stream at its base. Rising again on the far side, the path turns to follow the rim of the valley, passing the rocks seen as you climbed the ridge.

C As you pass the last of the formations, ignore a path off left and continue ahead, the way gently descending towards a clump of birch trees. Beyond, the path turns to fall more steeply, dropping through woodland back into Stain Dale. At the bottom of the hill, go ahead where a path joins from the left to a second junction a few yards on. Turn left, now retracing your steps to the car park. ●

The derivation of the name **'Bridestones'** is not certain, but is perhaps a corruption of 'Brinkstones' from the Norse language and referring to their position above the rim of the valley. An alternative theory, however, suggests that the rocks may have been the focus of an ancient fertility ceremony. And, of course, there is always a more romantic explanation; one story tells that a young couple, crossing the moor after their wedding, were suddenly engulfed in mist and sought temporary refuge amongst the rocks until it cleared.

? *Can you identify which of the stones is called the 'Pepper Pot'?*

4 St Gregory's Minster

Secluded in woodland at the foot of a steep gorge, the ancient church of St Gregory's Minster has a fascinating history. The unspoilt valley above winds for miles into the very heart of the moors, but you do not have to walk far to discover something of its serene beauty.

START St Gregory's Minster, Kirkdale

DISTANCE 2¼ miles (3.6km)

TIME 1½ hours

PARKING Roadside parking near St Gregory's Minster (not church car park)

ROUTE FEATURES Mainly woodland and field paths, with a short stretch along a quiet lane

A waymark by the junction at the head of the lane leading to the church indicates a bridlepath up a wooded banking. Emerging into a field at the top, turn right above Kirkdale Wood West. Part-way along the second field, cross into the trees before shortly emerging onto a lane.

A Turn right and follow the lane down through the wood, looking for a ruined lime kiln on your left. Eventually arriving at Hold Caldron, walk on past the front of the old mill and over a stone bridge spanning Hodge Beck.

B Just over the bridge, turn through a gate on the right onto a

The term 'minster' equates to 'mission', and it is possible that the first chapel here was an outpost associated with the 7th-century monastery at Lastingham. There was certainly a church here about 750, and two elaborately carved tombstones from its early period still lie inside the church. Perhaps the most remarkable relic, however, is an inscribed Saxon sundial, built into the south wall above the doorway. Inscribed in Old English, it commemorates the rebuilding of the church by Orm, son of Gamel in the days of King Edward and Earl Tostig, around 1060.

PUBLIC TRANSPORT Seasonal bus service past St Gregory's, bus service along main road (½ mile)

REFRESHMENTS None

PUBLIC TOILETS None

ORDNANCE SURVEY MAPS Explorer OL26 (North York Moors – Western Area)

The woodland floors are splashed with yellow primroses in spring

In a **cave**, discovered near the church in 1821, quarrymen found hundreds of bones and teeth. Examination showed them to be the remains of elephants, bears, tigers and other animals, thought to have been killed by hyenas some 70,000 years ago.

woodland track, which rises steadily through the trees. At a fork, bear left and continue climbing to a junction at the top.

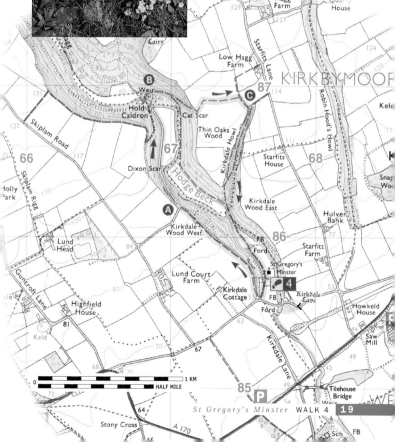

Go left, but then keep ahead to a stile out of the trees just above and walk away across the field beyond.

For much of the year, the river-bed by the church is quite dry, yet, beneath the bridge at **Hold Caldron** is an ample flow that once powered the corn mill there. The valley runs through limestone, and the waters disappear below ground soon after the bridge, running through a subterranean channel to emerge downstream.

C At the far side, follow the perimeter right to a stile, from which a path drops at the edge of trees to a track at the head of Kirkdale Howl. Turn sharp right and walk into a deepening wooded valley, keeping left at successive forks. Bear left at the bottom, the track running above the stream bed. Take the right branch at the next fork to emerge from the trees into a field. Keep ahead to a bridge over the watercourse and return to St Gregory's Minster. ●

What purpose did the steps that lie beside the lane near the church serve?

St Gregory's Minster

Rievaulx to Helmsley

Although described as a one-way walk, taking advantage of the seasonal Moors Bus service from the attractive old market town of Helmsley, the distance is not so great as to preclude making a day of it to complete the double journey. The route is pleasant throughout and there is much to see and do before and after the walk.

START Rievaulx Abbey
DISTANCE 3 miles (4.8km)
TIME 1¾ hours
PARKING Car parks at Helmsley (pay and display), then take seasonal bus to Rievaulx
ROUTE FEATURES Clear tracks and paths throughout and a short stretch along a country lane at the start

5

From the entrance to Rievaulx Abbey, follow the lane downstream by the River Rye to a junction beside Rievaulx Bridge. Turn left, crossing the flood plain to continue below the steep escarpment of Abbot Hag Wood. Just after the lane bends left to climb into Ingdale Howl, leave the lane onto a woodland track on the right, signed as the Cleveland Way to Helmsley.

A The way climbs steadily along the valley side through Quarry Bank Wood, later levelling to pass below disused quarry workings, which are now almost hidden by

Begun in 1132, **Rievaulx** was the first Cistercian monastery in northern England, founded by 12 monks from Clairvaux in France. Led by an English abbot, William, they faced a daunting task in clearing woodland, draining marshes, diverting rivers and constructing canals and fishponds to tame the 'vast solitude and horror' which an early writer ascribed to the valley. It took over 100 years to complete the abbey church and its attendant buildings, supporting at its peak, 140 monks and 600 lay brothers.

the lush vegetation. If you are not pressed for time, go left at a junction, a little farther on. A track leads to a field above, where grassy

PUBLIC TRANSPORT Bus service to Helmsley
REFRESHMENTS Choice of tea rooms and pubs in Helmsley
PUBLIC TOILETS Helmsley and at Rievaulx for visitors to the abbey
ORDNANCE SURVEY MAPS Explorer OL26 (North York Moors – Western Area)

Helmsley's 12th-century castle was built primarily for defence and has imposing earthwork embankments and a spectacular ruined keep. Inside, Tudor apartments contrast with the stark military architecture, and were built when comfort assumed a greater precedence. However, when Thomas Duncombe inherited the estate, he desired more than a draughty old castle, and in 1713, began work on a **fine new house**. Having survived two disastrous fires and 60 years as a girls' school, it has been superbly restored by the Duncombe family and is open to the public.

mounds and shallow ditches mark the site of an abandoned medieval village, Griff.

B Otherwise, continue ahead, the track now running at the edge of fields above Whinny Bank Wood. Beyond a gate at the far end, the way continues over open ground below Griff Lodge. Keep ahead across its drive on the continuation of the Cleveland Way. Shortly, after passing through a gate, the route drops steeply to negotiate a wooded valley, Blackdale Howl, climbing on the far side to emerge from the trees at the edge of expansive fields.

C An enclosed path takes the way on along the perimeter, eventually turning to climb around

Rievaulx Abbey

the far end. Through a gate at the top, go right onto a broad track, which gradually descends towards Helmsley. Readily spotted in the distance are the castle ruins and tower of All Saints' Church and, as you get closer, you can also see Helmsley's walled garden.

Eventually, the track ends by Helmsley's main car park, at a monument marking one end of the Cleveland Way. There, you can turn right to explore the castle and town, or carry on ahead, past Ryeburn Teashop selling delicious home-made ice cream, to the end of the street, where the 13th-century church lies to the right. ●

> **?** *What is the symbol used to denote the Cleveland Way?*

6 Kilburn White Horse

The best views of the White Horse are to be had from a mile or so away to the south-west, but it is an impressive sight even at close range. The cliff-top prospect towards the Vale of York is spectacular and, there is often the added treat of gliders soaring into the sky from the flying club just behind.

START White Horse, near Kilburn

DISTANCE 2¼ miles (3.6km)

TIME 1¾ hours

PARKING Car park at start of walk

ROUTE FEATURES Steep climb on stepped path at start, woodland paths and tracks, unguarded cliff edge

A forester at work in the Hood Hill Plantation

From the car park a steep flight of steps climbs beside the White Horse to the top of the scarp. To the left, a good path then follows the cliff edge around the perimeter of the airfield.

Ⓐ After ¾ mile (1.2km), at a red-topped marker post, go left onto a narrower path that doubles back in an oblique descent. On the way down, openings in the trees allow more splendid vistas across the plain and to the cliffs of Sutton Bank farther north before you eventually reach a broad track. Turn right, but almost immediately,

PUBLIC TRANSPORT Bus service to Kilburn (1½ miles)

REFRESHMENTS Picnic area by car park and Forresters' Arms in nearby Kilburn (1½ miles)

PUBLIC TOILETS Nearest at Sutton Bank Visitor Centre (1½ miles)

ORDNANCE SURVEY MAPS Explorer OL26 (North York Moors – Western Area)

Inspired by Thomas Taylor and cut by volunteers headed by the village schoolmaster, the turf figure at Kilburn is the only **white horse** in the north of England. Some 314 ft (96m) long and nearly 228 ft (69m) high, it is said two dozen people can sit on the grass left undisturbed for its eye. As the underlying rock is an unremarkable dull brown, limewash was applied to make it stand out. Today, however the villagers use chalk chippings instead when they give it a periodic spring clean.

leave sharp left along a marked bridleway that drops into the lower forest. Keep ahead when you later cross a green track, continuing your descent until you finally emerge onto a foresters' road.

B Walk just a short distance left to a green-topped marker post, and

The Kilburn White Horse is a local landmark

Born in 1876 in nearby **Kilburn**, Robert Thompson was the son of a carpenter and wheelwright. He developed a talent for woodcarving and soon achieved a reputation for producing fine oak furniture and ecclesiastical fittings. His trademark was a tiny carved mouse, which the craftsman worked into the decoration of every piece he made. Many of the local churches contain examples of Thompson's work, but his fame spread far beyond his native Yorkshire and you will even find the Mouseman's mark in Westminster Abbey. He died in 1955, but the workshop he founded continues in the village and his cottage is a showroom for its beautiful products.

there make an acute left turn onto a wide, rising path. After a sharp, right-hand bend, the ascent continues, shortly joining a higher track. With most of the climbing now behind you, follow it right, and then, when you reach a junction, go left. At another fork, just a little farther on, keep going along the right branch, which before long, emerges onto a picnic area below the car park.

> **In what year was the White Horse cut?**

Sutton Bank

7

START Sutton Bank National Park Visitor Centre

DISTANCE 2½ miles (4km)

TIME 2 hours

PARKING Car park at Visitor Centre (pay and display)

ROUTE FEATURES Woodland paths, unguarded cliff edge, prolonged ascent near end

For many visitors, the sharply-twisting, steep road negotiating Sutton Bank is the gateway to the North York Moors National Park. From the top, there is a magnificent view to Yorkshire's other National Park, the Dales. After following the cliff edge, this walk drops through attractive woodland to Gormire Lake, unusual in that no streams either feed or drain it.

William Wordsworth climbed **Sutton Bank** with his sister, Dorothy, in July 1802, during a journey to Brompton where his soon-to-be wife, Mary Hutchinson, lived. The breathtaking vista inspired the poet to write a sonnet, whilst Dorothy remarked in her journal on the cattle that were being herded from Scotland along the Hambleton Hills drove to be sold in the market at York.

Cross the picnic area behind the Visitor Centre to the junction of a lane with the main road at the top of Sutton Bank and follow a footpath opposite, signed 'Cleveland Way' and 'Sneck Yate',

At the top of the path from Gormire Lake

PUBLIC TRANSPORT Seasonal bus service

REFRESHMENTS Tea room and picnic area at Visitor Centre

PUBLIC TOILETS Beside Visitor Centre

ORDNANCE SURVEY MAPS Explorer OL26 (North York Moors – Western Area)

along the top of Sutton Brow. Initially in woodland, the way later emerges onto more open heath, giving some splendid views across the Vale of Mowbray. After ¾ mile (1.2km) the path loses height before turning right around the corner of the wall.

A A little farther on, leave, going sharp left onto a descending bridleway, signed 'Thirlby Bank'. After first falling across open heath, the route soon drops into woodland, winding steeply down through the trees along the course of a banked track. Ignore side paths until, eventually, you reach a junction at the bottom of the hill by a retrospective signpost to Thirlby Bank.

B Turn left onto a gently undulating track towards Gormire, the way confirmed a short distance along by a signpost. The lake soon comes into view, the path taking you to its shore, which, on a fine day, makes a grand spot for a picnic.

C At another signpost by the water's edge, turn away from the lake along a permissive path climbing through the trees towards Sutton Bank. Over a stile part-way up, keep on through Garbutt Wood until you reach a junction with a higher path. Go right, soon emerging into a clearing to pass a

Many fantastic stories are told about **Gormire**, several featuring a white horse, which accounts, in part, for the figure cut into the scar above Kilburn. One legend attributes the lake's creation to the Devil who, astride a galloping mount, plunged to earth off the cliff leaving behind a bottomless crater. A sadder tale describes the tragedy of a young maid, whose white mare slipped, carrying her over the cliff to her death in the lake.

large isolated boulder. Beyond, the gradient, having briefly eased, resumes its upward trend and a stiff pull to the top of Sutton Bank follows. Here, you rejoin the Cleveland Way. Turn right and follow it back to the Visitor Centre. ●

Look hard at the 'National Park tree' sculpture in the Visitor Centre foyer. What can you find worked into its branches?

The view from Sutton Brow

8

Spout House and Bilsdale

START Sun Inn on B1257 from Helmsley	
DISTANCE 3½ miles (5.6km)	
TIME 2 hours	
PARKING Beside Sun Inn (no charge, but the landlord asks that you buy some refreshment)	
ROUTE FEATURES Field paths and tracks, a short stretch on the road	

The 16th-century cruck-framed cottage that later became the original Sun Inn is the start point for this undemanding walk that follows the valley side to the tiny hamlet of Fangdale Beck. Break your journey there to wander down to the little church of St John before returning above the western bank of the river.

Walk through the farmyard and bear left beside a barn, leaving through a gate on the left. Head to another small gate at the far side and carry on across subsequent fields, making for the buildings of Hollin Bower Farm.

Originally built as a farmhouse in 1550, **Spout House** served as a hostelry for 200 years until the present Sun Inn opened in 1914. Remarkably, it has survived the centuries almost unchanged and gives a fascinating insight into the past.

A Over a ladder-stile, turn left, crossing a track to continue on a waymarked trail into the corner of a hillside enclosure. Follow the bottom boundary, later crossing a stile on the left, just before the corner. Cut right to another stile and maintain the same direction across the next field. Back in pasture, stick beside the top perimeter. Over yet another stile, walk on to a gate, and through that, bear left to a ladder-stile. Cross the next couple of fields above Low Crossett Farm to a gate by a large sycamore. Follow the hedge beside a copse, but where a

PUBLIC TRANSPORT Seasonal bus service
REFRESHMENTS Drinks only are available from the Sun Inn, but you are welcome to enjoy your own picnic at the tables outside
PUBLIC TOILETS Beside Sun Inn
ORDNANCE SURVEY MAPS Explorer OL26 (North York Moors – Western Area)

track develops, descending to High Crossett Farm, bear right above the buildings. Keep ahead over a broken wall and then drop left beyond the barns to a track.

B Follow it left past the farm, but at a left-hand bend, walk ahead at the edge of a field, emerging through its bottom hedge onto the road. Fangdale Beck lies to the left,

and to visit the church, carry on down the road. Otherwise, cut the corner by a footpath, a short way along on the right, which drops across a field to a footbridge over the River Seph. Go right into the hamlet.

C After 200 yds (183m) cross Fangdale Beck by a footbridge on the left and turn right along a track in front of a former Methodist chapel. Around a bend just beyond,

Inside Spout House

the route leads down the valley to Malkin Bower Farm. Walk ahead through the farmyard, leaving by a gate into the fields beyond. Keep going at the edge of subsequent fields, the way later running above the river. Through a gate just beyond there, across the valley from Spout House, turn right to

Lord Feversham, the local landowner, allowed the installation of the public telephone box by the road junction into the village of **Farndale Beck** on condition that it was painted green to harmonise with the landscape.

British Telecom ran into trouble when they replaced it with a glass box in 1992, for by then it had become a listed building and the company was fined and required to reinstate it.

climb the field edge before resuming your down-valley direction along the top wall to reach the next farm, Helm House.

D Again, carry on ahead, leaving along a track past barns and climbing to an enclosure where more barns stand on the left. Pass through gates between them to the field behind and follow its perimeter down towards the river. Leave at the bottom corner onto a track and, over a bridge, walk up to the road. Spout House is then a short walk to the left.

? *What animal's head is carved on the stone outside the Sun Inn?*

The Captain Cook Monument

High on the summit of Easby Moor, commanding fantastic views over the Cleveland plain and into Kildale, is a 60-foot obelisk erected to commemorate one of England's greatest seamen, Captain James Cook. The walk to it meanders through the forest that cloaks the hillside below before returning past one of the mining sites to be found in the area.

START Great Ayton Station
DISTANCE 4½ miles (7.2km)
TIME 3¼ hours
PARKING Beside station
ROUTE FEATURES Woodland paths and tracks, with a sustained climb from the start, which is steep towards the summit

9

From the station car park, return to the road, cross the bridge and then turn right along a track by a postbox. Carry on through a gate and then bear right over a stream and across a paddock to leave onto a track at the top. Turn left, and at its end, go right, climbing past a house and on at the edge of a wood. Continue beyond the trees and, through a gate and later over a stile, beside a rising wall.

The Cook Monument

A Where the path levels at the end of the wall, turn left and climb to a gate leading into a forest above. Through that, bear right and follow a steeply ascending path, continuing directly across a broad track, a little way up. Towards the top, a clearing on the left offers a magnificent vista across the valley to Roseberry Topping. Beyond there, the gradient eases and the path breaks from the trees, rising more easily

PUBLIC TRANSPORT Rail service, bus service to Great Ayton (¾ mile)
REFRESHMENTS Choice of pubs and cafes in Great Ayton
PUBLIC TOILETS Behind Captain Cook's Schoolhouse in Great Ayton
ORDNANCE SURVEY MAPS Explorer OL26 (North York Moors – Western Area)

across open heath to a junction. Turn right and walk on to the monument, which is now visible ahead.

B Carry on along a path from the obelisk's eastern face (the opposite one to that bearing the inscription), shortly descending at the edge of the heath before entering the forest. Where it later forks, take the right branch, signed 'Cleveland Way' and carry on until it joins a stone forest road. There, turn right on a path into the trees, which, on reaching the top of a steep bank, slopes down to the left, eventually ending at a lane.

C Follow it down through Bankside Farm, but at a sharp left bend, by a cottage below, leave onto a waymarked forest track climbing from a gate on the right. Where it shortly splits, keep ahead on the steadily rising track. Farther on, a clearing gives a grand view into Kildale and of the Cleveland Hills beyond. At another fork, not far beyond, follow the waymarked bridleway to the right, which soon

leads out of the trees. Continue ahead by a wall under the flank of Easby Moor, ignoring a path later signed off right, and eventually reaching a gate into a plantation. Carry on through to leave by another gate at the far side.

D A few paces ahead, fork left through a gate to follow a permissive bridleway that descends past the site of Ayton mines before dropping more steeply to a small reservoir. Carry on past a derelict building to follow a track above the railway. Reaching a junction at its end, go right through a gate, and then left over a stile to follow your outward track back to the station and the start of the walk. ●

Overlooking Kildale

Cook's school in **Great Ayton** now houses a fascinating exhibition of his life and outstanding achievements. Have a look, too, at the 12th-century All Saints' Church where, in the quiet graveyard, you will find the tombstones of his mother and five of his seven brothers. To see the cottage to which his parents retired, you must visit Australia, where it was taken in 1934. But marking the spot is an obelisk, fashioned out of rock cut from Point Hicks, Cook's first landfall in Australia on 20 April 1770.

Where and when did Captain Cook lose his life?

10 *Staithes*

START By Staithes harbour

DISTANCE 4½ miles (7.2km)

TIME 2¾ hours

PARKING Car park above old village (pay and display)

ROUTE FEATURES Exposed cliffs, field and woodland paths, moderate climb

From the narrow, twisting stone streets of picturesque Staithes, this walk follows the coast south to Port Mulgrave. The return lies through a pretty woodland nature reserve, rich in wild flowers and birds, before culminating in a spectacular view across the old village, where Cook developed his passion for the sea while working in William Sanderson's haberdashery and grocery shop.

With tiny cottages perched on the cliffs like nests in a seabird colony, it is hardly surprising that little room has been left in the old village for its streets and Dog Loup claims the title for the narrowest street in northern England. Until the advent of the steam trawler, **Staithes** lived by fishing, and in the 19th century, there were some 300 men sailing from here in small cobles, their catches being among the largest along the coast.

From the Cod and Lobster pub, leave up Church Street, passing Cook's Cottage and a small mission church. Continue on the Cleveland Way, shortly turning left to Runswick Bay. Beyond farm buildings, keep ahead across successive fields, eventually rising to a final stile to reach the cliff top.

Ⓐ Carry on at the field edge above sheer cliffs, climbing gently to the high point by Beacon Hill. Beyond, the way descends towards Port Mulgrave and, over a stile, continue along a narrow lane past cottages above the old harbour before turning away from the coast.

Ⓑ When you reach a telephone box, turn right towards a farm, progressing into a field at the end of the track. At a waymark walk

PUBLIC TRANSPORT Bus service

REFRESHMENTS Choice of pubs in Staithes and Fox and Hounds at Dalehouse

PUBLIC TOILETS Adjacent to car park

ORDNANCE SURVEY MAPS Explorer OL27 (North York Moors – Eastern Area)

left across and then follow a hedge to a stile in the corner. Descend at the edge of the next field and then go left above an embankment. Over another stile, lose height to emerge by St Hilda's

There is a fine view along the cliffs above Port Mulgrave

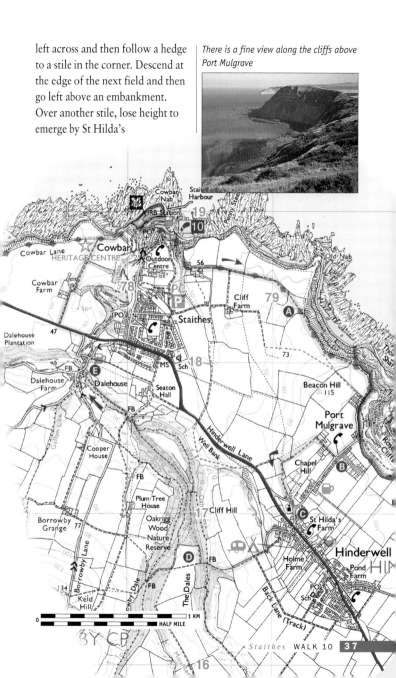

Church and follow the lane left to the main road.

C Cross into West End Close opposite and, at the bottom, walk right along Porret Lane, which degrades to a track. At a cottage, go right on a field track. Where it then turns left, continue ahead into the next field and on over stiles, soon dropping beside a wooded gully. Across a stream at the bottom, scale the opposite bank, emerging from the trees into an open field.

Tall houses emphasise the narrowness of Staithes' streets

D Turn right along its perimeter, returning to the trees in the corner. Ignore the obvious path descending right, and instead, bear left to find another path that falls more gradually along the crest of a narrowing ridge. When you reach a junction, walk ahead left on a well-made track on the opposite side of the ridge.

Leaving the trees, the way continues across open ground before dropping to a bridge by a

? *To whom is the small mission church in Staithes dedicated?*

small caravan site. Follow a track away beside the stream to Dalehouse.

E Go right through the hamlet to the Fox and Hounds. Turn left beside it and, over a bridge, climb right to the main road. After 200 yds (183m) up the hill, leave along a track to Cowbar Farm. Approaching the farmyard, bear right to a stile and follow a wall past the buildings to a former railway bridge. Beneath it, carry on across the field to a lane, which to the right, descends steeply through Cowbar to Staithes harbour. A short detour from a bend on the

Iron-rich cliffs overlooking a convenient landing brought industry to **Port Mulgrave** in the 1850s, and a harbour was completed in 1857, enabling the ore to be shipped to Tyneside. After the deposits were exhausted, a mile-long tunnel was dug through the cliffs for a mineral railway, connecting the port with iron mines at nearby Easington.

When the iron mines closed in 1930, the railway was dismantled, and after the outbreak of war, to prevent its use by invading German forces, the harbour pier was partly demolished.

way down leads onto Cowbar Nab, where there is a stunning view over the old village. ●

Small boats lie in the creek behind the harbour at Staithes

11 Robin Hood's Bay

START Robin Hood's Bay, above old town

DISTANCE 4½ miles (7.2km)

TIME 2¾ hours

PARKING Station Car Park (pay and display)

ROUTE FEATURES Coast path and disused railway line, unfenced cliffs, moderate climb

Described by Arthur Mee as one of the most astonishing sights along the Yorkshire coast, Robin Hood's Bay has long been popular with holiday-makers and walkers, and marks the end of the famous 'Coast to Coast' walk, that begins at St Bee's Head in Cumbria. After following the cliffs, the walk returns along the former coastal railway between Whitby and Scarborough.

🖌 Begin along Mount Pleasant North, which leaves the main road

No one really knows how the legendary **Robin Hood** became associated with this little fishing village; one of the few safe landings along the rocky and treacherous coast and which grew to prominence during the mid-16th century. Tales tell of him assisting the Abbot of Whitby repel Scandinavian raiders or giving help to the villagers who offered him a refuge from the law. But what is certain is that the place grew rich, not just from fishing, but by smuggling. The contraband was hidden in a network of secret tunnels and passages after being furtively shipped from France and the Low Countries.

almost opposite Station Car Park, signed 'Cleveland Way'. Where it bends left at the end, keep ahead in front of houses to a gate into Rocket Post Field. The way continues around its perimeter and on above the cliffs, giving views of the sweeping coastline to the north and south.

Ⓐ In due course, the path passes the foot of Rain Dale, where twin gullies bring streams to cascade over the precipitous edge. *A concessionary path to the abandoned railway climbs the ridge that separates them, providing a convenient link to the return route*

PUBLIC TRANSPORT Bus service

REFRESHMENTS Choice of pubs and cafes in Robin Hood's Bay

PUBLIC TOILETS Adjacent to car park

ORDNANCE SURVEY MAPS Explorer OL27 (North York Moors – Eastern Area)

if you wish to shorten the walk.
Otherwise, keep going above the
sheer cliffs, which, ahead, rise to
the highest point along the coastal
section of this walk. The onward
route is never in doubt,
eventually dipping to cross a
stream by a National Trust
marker 'Bottom
House Farm'.

The Bay Hotel overlooks the slipway

the left as you climb the field edge to a stile. Continue up the next field, leaving at its top-right corner.

C Now on the trackbed of the old railway, turn left and follow it back to Robin Hood's Bay, an easy stroll of

B Over the stream, leave the cliffs along the Centenary Path, which rises beside a wall above Limekiln Slack. The ruined lime kiln lies to some 1¾ miles (2.8km). Through a gate at its end, bear left into Mount Pleasant North to return to the car park.

> The **old town** is a maze of narrow streets and tiny cottages, clinging to the precipitous ground above the bay. At one time, 130 tiny, flat-bottomed cobles sailed from the shore in search of herring, cod, crab and lobster, despite facing ferocious storms and dangerous landings amongst the treacherous cliffs. Countless craft have been wrecked on the jagged rocks, but many lives were saved by the brave fishermen, crewing the town's lifeboat which was launched from the beach and powered only by oars. Those on land have often been threatened, too, as waves driven by savage gales attacked the soft cliffs. Over the years, many cottages and even roads have fallen into the sea.

Leave your vehicle in the car park while you wander down to explore the lower town and its expansive beach. Children will enjoy investigating the many rock pools exposed at low tide, and, if lucky, will find fossil ammonites and belemnites among the rocks washed out from the crumbling cliffs. *But, watch for rock falls, an ever-present danger, and incoming tides, which can cut off your retreat.*

> **?** *Why is Rocket Post Field so called?*

Forge Valley and the River Derwent

12

START Old Man's Mouth towards head of Forge Valley

DISTANCE 4 miles (6.4km)

TIME 2½ hours

PARKING Old Man's Mouth Car Park in Forge Valley

ROUTE FEATURES Initial steep climb. Also, 'easy going' riverside trail suitable for prams and wheelchairs

The deep ravine of Forge Valley is a geologically recent formation, gouged out by torrential glacial melt-waters at the end of the last ice age when the Derwent's original flow into the North Sea was blocked by a dam of ice near present-day Scalby. This walk wanders north from the gorge for a wonderful view of this unusual formation as the main valley splits into two.

With an atmosphere heavy with smoke and echoing to the clatter of the forges that would later give it its name, the **14th-century valley** was the scene of great industrial activity. Yet it was this smelting of ironstone, using charcoal from the forest, that helped preserve the woodland. The process required great quantities of charcoal and, although there was an abundancy of trees, indiscriminate felling would have rapidly exhausted them. Instead, the woodland was coppiced to produce a regular supply of small timber, and as you wander through today, you can still see the old boles of trees harvested in this way.

A footbridge, just behind the car park, provides a passage to a duck-boarded path along the Derwent's western bank. Follow it upstream, but after 40 yds (36m), turn off onto a permissive path, which zigzags up the otherwise impossibly steep valley side. Although the climb is sustained, the track is good and, before too long, emerges onto a level path running along the top edge of the valley.

A Turn sharp right above Scarwell Wood. Ignore a path shortly signed

PUBLIC TRANSPORT Bus service to East Ayton (1½ miles)

REFRESHMENTS Pub at East Ayton (1½ miles), picnic area beside car park

PUBLIC TOILETS None

ORDNANCE SURVEY MAPS Explorer OL27 (North York Moors – Eastern Area)

One of the best mixed **deciduous woodlands in the area**, it supports a rich diversity both in the plant and animal life. Come armed with a field guide to help you identify some of the many trees and flowering plants you will come across. Afterwards, drive up the valley to a bird-feeding station and sit quietly to be amazed at the number of species that come and go.

off left to Cockrah Road, and carry on behind a farm at Spikers Hill. Over stiles beyond the buildings, continue ahead at the field edge, joining a track that shortly descends into the trees along the side of the valley. As you lose height, occasional gaps in the trees give a view out to the coast.

B Emerging at the bottom of the forest, leave the track over a stile by gates into the field below and walk on up the valley. Gradually lose height from the fence, passing above

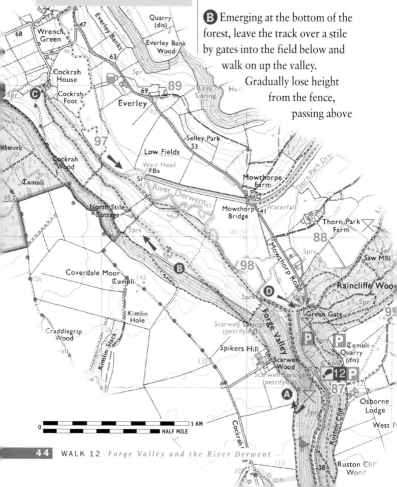

the isolated ruin of a stone barn and on beyond a stream to a small gate, part-way down the far hedge. Continue ahead across a dip, following a hedge up to a stile beside North Stile Cottages. Over that, walk on to join a track that leads away from the cottages up the valley to Cockrah House, a little less than ¾ mile (1.2km) away.

The path through Forge Valley beside the Derwent

C There, instead of following the track out over a cattlegrid, turn around to return along the valley, but now walking beside the bottom boundary of its open pasture. Across a stile by the Derwent, keep going in the base of the valley over successive fields, sometimes by the water's edge, but at other times, striking across to cut off the river's twisting passage. Eventually, the way joins the outgrown remnants of an old, sparse hedge at the edge of a banking above the flood meadow. At the far end, bear right, climbing beside a fence at the fringe of a wood to reach a stile.

D Once into the trees, follow a descending path back to the riverbank. Go right and head downstream, shortly returning to the bridge by the car park at Old Man's Mouth. ●

> **?** *What crustacean might you find living in the waters of the River Derwent?*

Rosedale

START	Rosedale Abbey
DISTANCE	3¾ miles (6km)
TIME	2¼ hours
PARKING	Car parks in village
ROUTE FEATURES	Field and woodland paths

At first sight, nothing remains of Rosedale's priory or iron mines, but look again. The church contains a nun's grave and ancient stone seat, while outside stands a ruined tower; miners' cottages were built from the priory's stones, and hillsides bear muted scars from old workings. An enjoyable ramble explores the peaceful valleys that converge on the village, and follows two delightful, babbling streams.

Even before the Romans arrived, **Rosedale** was known for its iron-rich rock, a resource later exploited by the nearby monastic communities. With the Industrial Revolution came new demands for iron, and when a vein of high-grade ore was discovered in 1851, a major industry developed. The village's population grew four-fold to almost 3,000 in just 20 years and by 1861, a railway was carrying the ore to the iron works. For almost 70 years, the boom continued, but after the First World War, decline set in and the last mine closed around 1926.

Walk past the Milburn Arms, signed 'Castleton', but immediately before a bridge across Northdale Beck, turn right. Over a stile at the top bear left, continuing above the stream. The way progresses naturally up the valley at the edge of successive fields, although not necessarily at the water's edge. Keep ahead when you later reach a signpost and again, soon after, past a field access bridge across the stream. Not far beyond, however, you will come to a footbridge where you should then cross the beck.

A Through a gate on the opposite bank, ignore a footpath climbing left, and walk through a gateway, marked 'Bridleway'. Follow a wall

PUBLIC TRANSPORT Seasonal bus service
REFRESHMENTS Choice of pubs and cafés in the village
PUBLIC TOILETS In village
ORDNANCE SURVEY MAPS Explorer OL26 (North York Moors – Western Area)

on your right above the stream until you emerge onto a lane. Cross to a gap opposite and continue in the same direction, steadily gaining height across the fields. After passing above a small reservoir and ruined farmstead, you meet a track by a gate. Instead of going through, turn back up

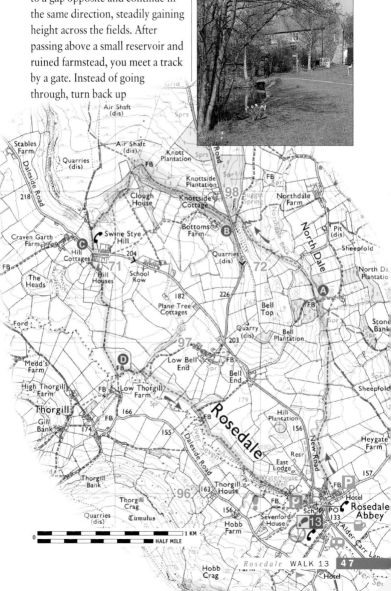

Many of Rosedale's cottages were built with stones from the former priory

the track, but a few steps on, climb the bank on the right to emerge through a gate onto a lane.

B Over a stile at a waymark 20 yds (18m) to the right, a path drops into a conifer plantation on the left. At a junction, keep ahead on a broad, level path. Farther on, after crossing a stream, the way bends left, subsequently losing height before emerging by Clough House. Over stiles, go right following the perimeter wall in front of the cottage and then, on the far side, pass through a gate to join a track leading away on the right. When you then reach a junction by a small barn, turn left and walk down to a lane by Hill Cottages.

C Cross to a track opposite that drops behind the houses and keep going downhill at the edge of a large field beyond its end. Through a gate at the bottom, turn right and walk downfield. Continue your descent into the valley across the subsequent fields until you reach a bridge over a stream.

D Instead of crossing, follow the field boundary left and through a gate. Bear left, crossing to a gap into the next field, where a field track leads right, up to a stile. Over that, walk ahead across successive fields, eventually returning to the water's edge beside another footbridge. Again, remain on this bank and keep ahead, passing from field to field above the river and later a camping site,

Looking along the valley towards Clough House

Rosedale bursts into colour with the coming of spring

Rosedale Abbey was actually a priory, founded around 1158 to house a small group of Cistercian nuns and dedicated jointly to St Mary and St Lawrence. Although it fell prey to Scottish raiders in 1322, the community actually prospered until it was dissolved in 1535 by order of King Henry VIII.

For some 300 years, the buildings were left to decay, but remained a substantial ruin until the mining boom of the 1850s. There was little thought of conservation in those days, and the ready-cut blocks of stone were plundered for building materials to be used in the rapidly expanding village of Rosedale.

before finally leaving through a kissing gate. A track leads ahead through the site, but at a children's play area, go left beside a house to a stile onto a lane. To the right, beyond a small cemetery, turn left on a path taking you to the church and on through a school play-ground back to the village centre.●

> **?** *How much did the Archbishop of York give to the rebuilding of St Lawrence's Church in 1839?*

14 *Hutton-le-Hole and Lastingham*

START Hutton-le-Hole
DISTANCE 4½ miles (7.2km)
TIME 2¾ hours
PARKING Car park at edge of village (charge)
ROUTE FEATURES Field paths and tracks, with short section on lane

Yorkshire has any number of captivating villages, but Hutton-le-Hole must be rated among the most charming; ancient cottages are set behind rolling greens where sheep still graze above a babbling stream. The pleasant walk crosses the fields to nearby Lastingham where the church has a beautiful crypt, beneath which lie the bones of one of the early Celtic missionaries, St Cedd.

The track to Grange Farm lies across open fields

From the car park, turn left and then left again to walk down the main street. Immediately after crossing a bridge at the far side of the village, leave to follow Fairy Call Beck upstream. Beyond a stile, bear away from the water's edge, following a contouring path around Austin Head and into a bracken-clad gully. At a waymark, strike left up the bank, passing through a gate and on to a break in an overgrown hedge. Continue uphill along an old track.

A At the top, the track bends left and then right around the edge of a

PUBLIC TRANSPORT Seasonal bus service
REFRESHMENTS Inn and tea shops at Hutton-le-Hole and Blacksmiths Arms in Lastingham
PUBLIC TOILETS Adjacent to car park
ORDNANCE SURVEY MAPS Explorer OL26 (North York Moors – Western Area)

field, to then head almost due east for nearly ½ mile (800m) over the crest of the hill. Reaching its end, walk left and then right by some barns and on to Grange Farm. Leave the fields through a gate and pass between barns to emerge onto a lane.

B Just to the right at a junction, turn left to walk through Spaunton, eventually dropping to another junction beyond the village. Go right, but then immediately leave onto a waymarked path on the left. Through a gate, it descends a wooded gully, continuing as a track at the bottom into Lastingham. Keep ahead past cottages overlooking a stream, and after crossing a bridge turn left. At the next junction, by a telephone box, go left again to St Mary's Church.

The first church at **Lastingham** was built in 654, when St Cedd, invited by King Ethelwald, came from Lindisfarne to found a new monastic community. He eventually became a bishop, but died of plague in 664. St Mary's marks the site of the early monastery, and was begun in 1078 when Stephen, formerly Abbot of Whitby, re-founded the community under the Benedictine Order. The crypt is unique in this country, having a nave, aisles and chancel, and its wonderful atmosphere is full of peace and spirituality.

C Return to the junction by the telephone box and turn left, climbing out of the village and, through a gate at the top, onto the moor. Before reaching a stone cross, a little farther on, go through a kissing gate on the left and follow a wall downhill.

One of Lastingham's delightful cottage gardens

Carry on over a stile to ford a brook and continue by the wall up the opposite bank. Where it ends, keep ahead across moorland to join a track leading away from Camomile Farm. It shortly curves to the left, eventually emerging onto a lane by Mary Magdalene Well.

D Follow the lane right for ½ mile (800m), leaving at a waymark onto a track that rises above the road and soon leads to a gate into a small wood. A descending path re-crosses Fairy Call Beck at the bottom, leading to a field beyond. Keep walking ahead across a succession of fields, finally winding between a churchyard and Hutton's bowling green to return to the village. The car park lies to the right, beyond the folk museum. ●

Make time to visit Hutton's **open-air folk museum**, where more than a dozen historic buildings have been rebuilt, rescued from the surrounding area. From humble cruck-frame cottages, to an Elizabethan manor house, the collection includes a village shop, blacksmith's forge and work-sheds. There is even a Victorian photographer's studio to explore. Together with many other fascinating exhibits, they portray aspects of moor and dale life over the centuries, showing how people earned their living, with regular demonstrations of traditional crafts and activities.

? *Can you find two wells in Lastingham dedicated to the saints associated with the monastery?*

Nunnington

START Caulkleys Bank, south of Nunnington

DISTANCE 4¾ miles (7.6km)

TIME 3 hours

PARKING Roadside lay-by above Caulkleys Bank

ROUTE FEATURES Field tracks and paths

Although just outside the National Park boundary, the gentle countryside around Nunnington is none the less attractive and the village has an interesting manor house to visit. Following a broad ridge, the walk gives fine views to the moors in the north and the Howardian Hills to the south, before returning along the River Rye to pass a substantial old mill.

Begin this walk along a track beside the parking area, heading east to pass a small copse along the top of Caulkleys Bank. After shortly passing a trig point, a long, gradual descent leads to a crossing track. Turn left, but then immediately right down another track, Caulkleys Lane.

A Emerging onto a lane at the bottom, go left to a junction and then right, signed 'Welburn' and 'Kirkbymoorside'. Walk down past West Ness Farm towards Ness Bridge.

Nunnington's peacocks are fascinating, whatever your age

PUBLIC TRANSPORT Bus service

REFRESHMENTS Tea room at Nunnington Hall and the Royal Oak in Nunnington village

PUBLIC TOILETS For visitors to Nunnington Hall

ORDNANCE SURVEY MAPS Explorer OL26 (North York Moors – Western Area)

Saxon farmers built the first **mill** here, but the present four-storey building was erected in 1875 at a cost of £700, which included the water wheel and milling machinery. It continued grinding into the 20th century and was subsequently used to generate power for **Nunnington Hall** until mains electricity was installed in the village in 1950.

B Immediately before it, cross into the field on the left and carry on upstream by the River Rye at the edge of successive fields. Soon after passing through a small gate, look for a stile on the right. The way continues for a short distance outside the field boundary to a second stile. Over that, walk ahead, cutting off a bend in the river, to the far right-hand corner of the enclosure. Across another stile there (ignore the nearby gate) keep going to Mill Farm.

Attractive cottages line the street as you climb through Nunnington

0   1 KM
HALF MILE

Ford

River Rye

Ness Bridge

Farm

Ness Cottages
49

West Ness Hall

West Ness

Ness Farm

Weir

B

A

Ness Hall

Highfield House

Ppg Sta

68

69

56

Caulkleys Lane

Quarry Plantation

Stampers Wood

78

Caulkleys Grange

farmhouse. Follow the course of the mill race to a stile by the weir. Bear left across the next field to a field gate just left of the end of a high wall surrounding Nunnington Hall. Through it, continue beside the grounds of the house, leaving the field by a stile after passing an estate cottage beyond. Turn left and walk out to a lane.

C Leaving the field, walk on through the farmyard and past the mill to a stile, right of the

> The **13th-century church** contains a fine funerary monument, once thought to represent a wandering knight, Sir Peter Loschy. Legends tells that a terrible dragon oppressed the village, and Sir Peter determined to slay it. As he hacked pieces from the beast during a hard-fought battle on nearby Loschy Hill, his dog buried them in a field above the church. The nobleman finally won the day and his faithful companion ran to lick his master's face, but the dragon's blood was poison, and both tragically died on their field of victory.

D Go right, but before you reach a bridge in front of the hall, turn left through the village. At the far end of the street, go left again, climbing past the Royal Oak to a junction beside the church.

E Opposite, a bridleway rises across the fields. On reaching the crest, turn left along an avenue of young Scots pine, which returns you to the parking area above Caulkleys Bank.

> **?** *Where can you find mice in the Church of All Saints and St James?*

16 *Byland Abbey*

START Jerry Carr Bank, west of Ampleforth

DISTANCE 4¾ miles (7.6km)

TIME 3 hours

PARKING Roadside lay-by beside Carr Lane

ROUTE FEATURES Field and woodland paths with steep climb out of Wass

Following part of the National Park boundary, this walk wanders across open fields to the spectacular ruins of Byland Abbey, returning through Wass and the woodland above the village. You might also visit the working abbey at nearby Ampleforth, which is sometimes open to visitors. It was founded in 1802 under the Benedictine Order, and the late Cardinal Hulme studied there.

At a waymark, a short way down-hill from the lay-by, turn into the field on the left. Follow a diagonal route, maintaining your direction across subsequent fields to reach a footbridge. Now bear right to the top corner and carry on over a hill, keeping well left of a barn. Pass through a waymarked gate in the far, bottom corner, from which a track leads towards Wass Grange.

A Entering a field by the farm, leave the track. Head across to the opposite boundary and turn left, continuing beyond its end to a power-line post on the hill side. There, go right, the overhead cables guiding you to a stile. About 100 yds (91m) along the left-hand hedge, cross another stile and bear right. A sign to Byland Abbey directs you up the field edge, the ruins appearing as you crest the rise.

PUBLIC TRANSPORT Bus service to Wass (alternative start)

REFRESHMENTS Abbey Inn opposite Byland Abbey and Wombwell Arms at Wass

PUBLIC TOILETS Behind Abbey Inn for visitors to abbey

ORDNANCE SURVEY MAPS Explorer OL26 (North York Moors – Western Area)

Byland Abbey was founded in 1177 by 12 Cistercian monks, who had left Furness Abbey in Lancashire some 40 years earlier in search of a new home. Its spiritual reputation flourished and the monastic house soon became known as one of the 'three luminaries of the north'. At its peak, during the 13th century, it supported a community of 36 monks and 100 lay brethren.

B Reaching a ruined barn, turn right and walk downfield, through a gate and on beside an outgrown hedge. At a waymark, pass through a gap and continue in the same direction along the adjacent field. Keep going beyond another gap to the abbey's perimeter fence. Turn right, cross a stile and walk ahead to emerge over a final stile onto a lane.

The fringes of Abbey Wood

C The abbey entrance lies to the left, but return to this point to resume the walk, continuing along the drive opposite to Abbey House Farm. Just a few paces along, cross a stile into a paddock on the right. Bear left to another stile on the far side and continue on a diagonal to a kissing gate at the far, top corner by Abbey Bank Wood. Maintain the same direction across the next field, leaving through a small gate to follow a track out to a lane. Turn right into Wass.

D At a junction by the Wombwell Arms, go left up Wass Bank.

Opposite the last house on the right, leave along an unmarked path on the left, which drops to a footbridge over a brook. Bear right up the bank into forest to join a track, climbing parallel with the lane. Where it narrows higher up, keep ahead over a rise and then drop right, re-crossing the stream to rejoin the lane.

E A farther ¼ mile (400m) up the hill, just before the gradient eases, turn right onto a track that leads across fields to a house. There, climb into the field on the left and follow its right-hand fence down to a stile at the corner, from which a winding path continues through woodland. Emerging from the trees, head right down to High Woods Farm and go right at the bottom along the field, with Low Wood over to your left. After crossing two fence lines, bear left off the track, following the perimeter of the wood to a stile at the enclosure's far end.

F Ahead, a winding and sometimes indistinct path falls easily through the trees, eventually descending a steep bank to a waymark. Turn right, shortly leaving the wood. Once more in open fields, walk down to a footbridge in the left hedge and continue across the field beyond. Over a crossing track leading to Carr House, keep going, eventually rising to a stile. The way then follows the woodland edge to another stile and plank bridge. Now

bear right, leaving at the far corner onto Carr Lane. The lay-by from which you began lies a short distance up the hill. ●

? *What was used to pave the floor of the great abbey church?*

Beautiful patterned floor tiles are one of the abbey's distinctive features

17 *Ravenscar*

START Ravenscar
DISTANCE 5¾ miles (9.3km)
TIME 3½ hours
PARKING Roadside parking by coastal centre
ROUTE FEATURES Moorland tracks and disused railway line

Although quite a long walk, setting out from the coast to cross the open moor before returning along the disused course of the former Whitby to Scarborough railway and passing the site of abandoned alum workings, the route is neither strenuous nor difficult and the little bit of climbing involved is completed soon after the start.

Follow a descending track from the coastal centre, which shortly turns beside a cutting that

Wide streets and isolated grand houses suggest **Ravenscar** is not all it might seem. In 1895, led by John Septimus Bland and encouraged by the success of the new railway, a consortium of Yorkshire businessmen planned a fashionable resort. Centred on a square by the railway station, they laid out streets and drains to serve some 1,200 houses. Perhaps because of the bleak, windswept location or the lack of an attractive beach, the scheme failed to catch the public imagination and few buildings were ever built.

PUBLIC TRANSPORT Bus service
REFRESHMENTS Bar snacks and meals at Raven Hall Hotel and Fox Cliffe Tea Rooms on Station Road
PUBLIC TOILETS At start of walk
ORDNANCE SURVEY MAPS Explorer OL27 (North York Moors – Eastern Area)

once carried the railway. Cross onto the old trackbed and continue to a bridge, leaving immediately beyond by steps up the bank. A track leads away from the bridge to a waymark, some 50 yds (46m) along, where you should turn sharp right through a gate into a rough field. Follow a diagonal line up the field, passing a cottage to a gate in the wall above. Head directly up the next field, leaving onto a lane in front of a cottage.

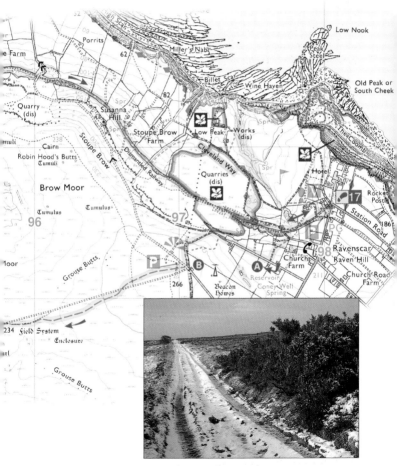

Snow adds its own beauty to the moor

Along the coast to Robin Hood's Bay

A Walk along to the right, the way gently rising as a track beyond

A necessary chemical in tanning and dyeing as well as being used in the manufacture of candles and parchment, **alum** was discovered in the North Yorkshire shales, and Ravenscar was one of some 30 places along the coast where it was dug. Quarrying began in 1640 and a processing plant was built to extract the salt. The industry collapsed when an alternative source was discovered, involving the treatment of colliery waste with sulphuric acid, and the works closed in 1862.

a farm. At the crest, immediately beyond a thoughtfully placed seat, fork left onto a narrow footpath that rises beside the boundary of a heather-clad hillside, climbing above a bridleway that leaves the track just a few yards farther on. Higher up, at a waymark, turn left to continue the ascent along a deeply sunken path. The gradient soon eases, the way passing a transmitter mast to a lane.

B A waymarked bridleway opposite leads across the open moor. After a mile, the track forks, the left branch avoiding a very boggy area a short way ahead. The two paths meet again beyond it and then immediately split again. Continue ahead along the right branch, still marked as a bridleway. The path now falls more noticeably, eventually ending at a junction in front of a farm at Cook House.

C A concrete track is signed right to How Dale and follows the edge of the moor back towards the coast. Ignore the turnings off to the left, but notice two low mounds in the adjacent fields, which are burial barrows. Eventually, the track turns left through a gate, heading down across fields to a wood before going right to Howdale Farm.

D Follow the track through gates and round below the front of the farmhouse, bearing left beyond to continue downhill at the edge of a deep wooded valley. Some 200 yds (183m) below the farm, where overhead cables cross the track, turn right onto a narrow path dropping steeply through the trees to a bridge over a stream at the bottom. In the field beyond, climb ahead, passing a waymark to reach a stone stile at the top. Keep going through trees and then across a shale bank to a track in front of a

Raven Hall was built in 1774, the country mansion of Captain William Childs who owned the alum quarries. A later owner, Dr Francis Willis, rose to fame as physician to Europe's royalty, and treated King George III when he developed his 'madness', possibly in this very house. Since 1895 it has been run as an hotel, its rooms and terraces enjoying grand views of the coast.

cottage, the former How Dale school. Follow it left, but beyond the next cottage, go through the first of two gates on the left down to Browside Farm. Bear left behind the buildings to the old railway track.

E Turn right and enjoy the easy walk back above the coast. After a mile, a path leaves over a stile on the left, dropping across the fields to the ruins of the Low Peak Alum Works. If you do walk down to have a look at them, bear in mind that you will have to climb back. The quarries lie farther along the track, where there is also a ruined brick kiln. It is then not much farther to the end of the walk. ●

Near the beginning of the walk is a wooden sculpture – what does it depict?

18 Hole of Horcum

START Newton Dale Halt

DISTANCE 5 miles (8km)

TIME 3¾ hours

PARKING Car parks at both Pickering and Grosmont (pay and display), take train to Newton Dale Halt (check return times from Levisham Station)

ROUTE FEATURES Moorland paths with a steep climb at the start, unguarded cliff edge

As well as stunning scenery, the North York Moors have one of the finest steam railways in the country. This walk brings them together, linking Newton Dale Halt and Levisham Station by a route through one of the Moors' most spectacular natural features. Take the first morning train from either Pickering or Grosmont to ensure you have ample time.

Leave the station and, beneath the railway bridge, turn left and follow Pickering Beck upstream below the embankment. After a couple of stiles, the path crosses the stream and heads away by a fence at the edge of Pifelhead Wood. Cross the fence over another stile higher up and continue into a narrowing gully. Steps ease the way up the steepest stretch, but the ascent is soon completed, and quite suddenly ends at the moor above.

A As you then go left above Yewtree Scar, there is a magnificent view into Newton Dale. Continue beside a fence farther on to reach a wall and there bear right, following it away from the cliffs towards buildings visible in the middle distance. Where the wall later ends, keep ahead above the

The Saltersgate Inn has an intriguing history. Once called the 'Wagon and Horses', it takes its present name from the fact that it lay on a packhorse route along which salt was conveyed inland from saltpans on the Tees estuary. Tales relate the gruesome murder of a customs official, sent to investigate suspected smuggling. His body was reputedly buried beneath the hearth, and the fire is never allowed to die out, for fear of his ghost re-appearing.

PUBLIC TRANSPORT Bus service to Pickering, main line rail service to Grosmont

REFRESHMENTS Saltersgate Inn near Hole of Horcum

PUBLIC TOILETS At main stations and on some trains

ORDNANCE SURVEY MAPS Explorer OL27 (North York Moors – Eastern Area)

Levisham Station marks the end of the walk

shallowing valley of Havern Beck, shortly reaching a stile by a gate. Carry on towards Glebe Farm and, over a couple more stiles, leave past it along a track, which joins the main road beside the 'Legendary Saltersgate Inn'.

B Across the carriageway to the right, a path leaves over a stile, climbing steeply right through a conifer plantation above the road. Towards the top, bend left, and after a final, short pull, leave the trees and rejoin the road at the top of the bank, where there is a stunning view across the Hole of Horcum. Now, follow the roadside down to the hairpin bend.

C Drop to a stile on the left, from which a path descends into the Hole. Continue through a gate and on below an isolated cottage, Low Horcum. Beyond there, bear away from the path rising towards the woodland ahead, and carry on

This spectacularly massive **amphitheatre**, some 300 ft (91m) deep, was created at the end of the ice age by torrential melt-waters carrying debris released by the retreating ice. Its striking appearance has given rise to all manner of legends as to the Hole's creation, one attributing it to a local giant called Wade, who, enraged over some domestic matter, scooped up a handful of earth and threw it at his nigglesome wife.

across the open pasture beneath the bank. Farther on, where the track again heads into the wood, keep right on the grassy swathe to a stile. Over it, the valley narrows, the path progressing along a steepening slope above the wooded stream, eventually dropping to a footbridge.

D Go over a second bridge just ahead and then turn right at a signpost to follow the tributary stream into Dundale Griff. The path rises easily alongside the base of the wooded valley, later emerging onto heather moor. When you reach a fork, bear right to remain in the shallow depression

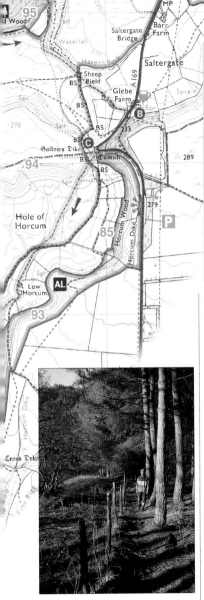

The railway from Whitby to Pickering opened in 1836, one of the country's earliest lines. Engineered by **George Stephenson**, it was designed originally for horse-drawn carriages, which looked more like stagecoaches than railway carriages. Above Beck Hole, carriages were hauled up an incline, but once over the watershed, they freewheeled down Newton Dale, reportedly reaching speeds of 30 miles per hour. The line was an immediate success and within 11 years, had been converted to steam. It closed in 1965, but, thanks to the hard work of dedicated enthusiasts, regular services resumed in 1973.

that is the head of the valley, making for a signpost, which appears just below the skyline.

E At the junction, the path ahead is signed to the station and leads past Dundale Pond, shortly to reach another junction by the corner of a wall. Again go forward, with the wall on your left, and, beyond its end, continue to the lip of a steep bank above Newton Dale. A sloping track leads left to the road below, where you can cut across its hairpin bend before following it down to Levisham Station.

Walking through Pifelhead Wood by Newton Dale Halt

? *Who made Dundale Pond?*

19 *Around Pickering Beck*

START Pickering
DISTANCE 5½ miles (8.9km)
TIME 3¼ hours
PARKING Several car parks in town (pay and display)
ROUTE FEATURES Good paths and tracks through both woodland and fields

Legend tells of the lost ring of King Peredurus being found inside a pike caught in the river here, and that he named the place 'pike-a-ring' in honour of the extraordinary event. This longer walk wanders the wooded valley above the town, but it should still leave you time to explore Pickering's other attractions.

The walk starts outside Beck Isle Folk Museum, from where you

Once owned by William Marshall, an 18th-century agricultural pioneer, **Beck Isle** houses a fine rural life museum. Every aspect of local activity over the past 200 years is illustrated in fascinating displays and life-like room settings. Wander into a Victorian drawing room, peek into a cottage parlour and visit the barber's shop, cobbler's and a working print room. Call at the chemist and grocery shops and see the 19th-century bar of the Station Hotel. Outside is an amazing collection of agricultural and forestry implements, tracing the often-ingenious mechanisation of many farming activities.

should head towards the centre of town and at the junction there, turn left into Park Street. Just beyond the front of the station, fork right along Castle Road, which rises towards the castle, the entrance to which is up steps to the right.

A Drop below its stark outer walls to rejoin the main road, and walk on beyond the castle. Ignore a footpath signed off right at the edge of a wood. Instead, continue a little farther to an unmarked path forking into the trees, which undulates parallel to the road. Disregard paths off right, but keep

PUBLIC TRANSPORT Bus and rail services
REFRESHMENTS Choice of pubs and tea rooms in town centre
PUBLIC TOILETS In the town and at places of interest
ORDNANCE SURVEY MAPS Explorer OL27 (North York Moors – Eastern Area)

ahead, eventually returning to the road just south of Newbridge.

B Walk on a few steps before leaving again along a broad track to Lowther House. A gate beyond the building takes the way into Pickering Forest as a woodland track at the bottom of a steep wooded bank. Ignore paths off, but keep going for about ½ mile (800m), eventually reaching a stile. Clamber out to the edge of a flood meadow and turn right above Pickering Beck along a narrow, open swathe, closed at its far end by the forest. A clear track continues through the trees, later crossing a tributary stream before

Founded in 1069 by William the Conqueror, **Pickering's Castle** was one of several northern fortifications, established to enforce an unwelcome Norman rule upon this distant part of his kingdom. The central mound or motte, surrounded by earthwork ditches was initially defended by a wooden palisade, today's ruined stone walls and buildings only appearing in the 12th century as military architecture and the resources to support more elaborate constructions developed. Although besieged by Robert the Bruce in the 14th century the castle survived until badly damaged during the Civil War. The great hall and chapel remain, as does much of the outer curtain wall, and the imposing shell of the central keep still dominates the town.

Farm implements on show in the Beck Isle Museum

reaching a footbridge over the main river.

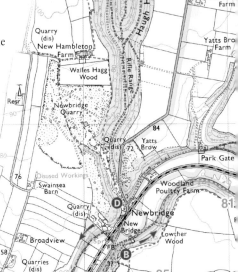

C On the opposite bank, walk ahead to the railway. Check it is safe before crossing and carry on to a broad track above. To the left, it leads beside the railroad back towards Pickering. Keep ahead where it is later joined by another track from the right, eventually emerging from the forest at Park Gate. Now metalled, the way continues past a farm and some railway maintenance yards before meeting the road at Newbridge.

D Turn left, go over the level-crossing and the river beyond before leaving the road 100 yds (91m) farther on to a footbridge on the right. Past the end of a terrace, re-cross the

Who owns Pickering Forest?

Spare the time to visit **Pickering's parish church**, which contains exquisite frescoes depicting scenes of martyrdom and biblical events. They date from the mid-15th century and, like medieval pictorial windows, were a teaching aid to instruct a largely illiterate congregation. Hidden by whitewash for much of their life, they are remarkably well-preserved, and display a wonderful vividness.

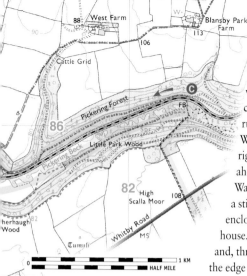

track. Beyond a couple of small paddocks, it continues below a wooded bank, past a cottage and then by the ruin of a large lime kiln. When it then bends sharply right, leave through a gate ahead into a grass field. Walk across, bearing right to a stile, over which an enclosed path leads past a house. Carry on over its drive and, through a kissing gate, at the edge of a rough field. Through another gate at the far side, continue beside an unkempt hedge, soon joining a track, which returns you to the town beside the museum. ●

railway, again exercising caution and carry on by more cottages before turning left onto a gated

The outer walls of Pickering Castle

Farndale

START Low Mill, Farndale

DISTANCE 6 miles (9.7km)

TIME 3¾ hours

PARKING Car park at Low Mill (charge)

ROUTE FEATURES Field paths and moorland tracks, sustained but not strenuous climb

During early April, Farndale's open woodland beside the winding Dove is resplendent with a carpet of yellow, as countless daffodils burst into flower. But at any other season, it is a wonderful place, and makes a fitting end to this longer, but generally easy walk, that explores the heather moor of Rudland Rigg, where you will often hear the gabbling calls of the red grouse.

Turn right out of the car park and follow the lane north up the valley. After ¼ mile (400m), leave through a gate on the left, along a track signed as a bridleway to Rudland Rigg. When you reach Horn End Farm, walk on beside it and then bear left on a track through the fields beyond. Keep going ahead through successive

The walk ends along Farndale

gates, the route taking you into West Gill below Horn Ridge. Before long, beyond High Barn, the way approaches West Gill Beck. Carry on above it to find a bridge across.

Ⓐ Climb away beside a wall, crossing it by a stile higher up. Continue on a faint path diverging

PUBLIC TRANSPORT None

REFRESHMENTS Seasonal café at High Mill and pub near route at Church Houses

PUBLIC TOILETS At car park

ORDNANCE SURVEY MAPS Explorer OL26 (North York Moors – Western Area)

The postman pays an early morning call to Low Mill Post Office

from the wall and rising to meet a clear track at a signpost. There, go right, through a gate and on, comfortably gaining height towards the head of the valley. Where the path later forks by a waymark, keep right, shortly passing a string of grouse butts. Beyond them, the path then kicks left to tackle the last few feet of ascent. When you reach a wide crossing track, turn right and follow it along the broad spine of Rudland Rigg.

B Before covering ½ mile (800m), you will reach a prominent cross-roads, where you should turn sharp right. The way leads back across the head of West Gill before

beginning a gradual descent into Farndale. Farther on, as the gradient becomes more purposeful, ignore a track off right, and soon leave the moor, dropping through a gate to continue down a rough field, finally reaching a lane at the bottom, opposite Monket House. Turn right and walk down to a junction **C**.

*If you want to call at the Feversham Arms at Church Houses, you will have to make a small detour, following the lane left into the bottom of the valley. To rejoin the main route at **D** follow a track, signed to Low Mill, which you will find on the right, immediately in front of the pub.*

The map shows locations including Penny Hill Crag, Penny Hill, Broom Hill (186), Grouse Butts, Quarry (dis), Dickon Howe, Wilson House (dis), Monket House, Monket House Crags (238), West Gill Slack, West Gill Head, Sheepfold, Quarry (dis), FARNDALE WEST CP, Grouse Butts, Field System, Horn Ridge, Hawthorn Crag, Cairn, Golden Heights, Tips (dis), Earthwork, Tumulus, Horn End Crag, West Gill, High Barn, Quarry (dis), Double Crag, Crow Wood, Scarth Nick, Garnets, Keys. Markers B, C, A, D are shown.

Bleak, wind-swept moors and isolated valleys emphasise the elemental forces of nature, and it is hardly surprising that beliefs in the **supernatural** and the 'other world' have been strong in these tightly-knit dale communities. Stories of hobgoblins abound, the little people who emerge under the cover of darkness to work mischief or provide help, as they saw befitting the behaviour of their mortal companions. A tale tells of Obtrusch, who lived on **Rudland Rigg** and so plagued one of Farndale's farmers that he was forced to pack his few belongings on a cart and abandon his farmstead to escape the vindictive tormentor. 'Ah see thoo's flittin' called a neighbour as he left, and the farmer turned pale as he heard a disembodied squeak from beneath the cart, 'Aye we're flittin'. The hobgoblin was never going to let him alone.

Otherwise, keep ahead at the junction and continue down the road. After 200 yds (183m), just before a wooden bench, go over a stile on the left, signed 'Church Houses'. Walk down, crossing a stile to reach a bridge over the River Dove at the bottom. In a small pasture on the other side, bear right, leaving over a stile onto a track opposite the café at High Mill **D**.

Follow the track between the cottages, passing through a gate

Now protected within a nature reserve that was created in 1953, **Farndale's wild daffodils** have heralded spring in the valley for centuries, and are known locally as 'Lenten Lilies', since their flowering often coincides with Easter. Until the 16th century, wild daffodils were common in woodlands throughout the country, although local stories attribute these to being planted either by the monks of Rievaulx Abbey or to the martyr, Nicholas Postgate, a 17th-century Catholic priest who was brutally executed for baptising a baby.

enclosure, bear right to pass through the lower of two gates in the far boundary. Twisting and weaving, the river snakes its way down the valley, and while the path does not always follow its bank, the way is well-trodden and never in doubt. Another mile (1.6km) of easy walking ultimately leads you over a bridge and back to the car park. ●

into a small meadow beyond. Carry on, generally ahead and progressing from one field to the next. At the far end of the third

? *What is the penalty for picking Farndale's daffodils?*

Looking towards the head of West Gill

Further Information

Walking Safety

Always take with you both warm and waterproof clothing and sufficient food and drink. Wear suitable footwear, i.e. strong walking boots or shoes that give a good grip over stony ground, on slippery slopes and in muddy conditions. Try to obtain a local weather forecast and bear it in mind before you start. Do not be afraid to abandon your proposed route and return to your starting point in the event of a sudden and unexpected deterioration in the weather.

All the walks described in this book will be safe to do, given due care and respect, even during the winter. Indeed, a crisp, fine winter day often provides perfect walking conditions, with firm ground underfoot and a clarity of light unique to that time of the year.

The most difficult hazard likely to be encountered is mud, especially when walking along woodland and field paths, farm tracks and bridleways - the latter in particular can often get churned up by cyclists and horses. In summer, an additional difficulty may be narrow and overgrown paths, particularly along the edges of cultivated fields. Neither should constitute a major problem provided that the appropriate footwear is worn.

Follow the Country Code

- Enjoy the countryside and respect its life and work
- Guard against all risk of fire
- Take your litter home
- Fasten all gates
- Help to keep all water clean
- Keep your dogs under control
- Protect wildlife, plants and trees
- Keep to public paths across farmland
- Take special care on country roads
- Leave livestock, crops and machinery alone
- Make no unnecessary noise
- Use gates and stiles to cross fences, hedges and walls

(The Countryside Agency)

Useful Organisations

Council for the Protection of Rural England
128 Southwark St,
London, SE1 0SW.
Tel. 020 7981 2800

Council for National Parks
246 Lavender Hill, London
SW11 1LJ.
Tel. 020 7924 4077

Countryside Agency
John Dower House, Crescent
Place, Cheltenham GL50 3RA.
Tel. 01242 521381

English Heritage
23 Savile Row, London W1X 1AB.
Tel. 0171 973 3250;
Fax 0171 973 3146;
www.english-heritage.org.uk

Regional Office
Yorkshire and the Humber
Tel. 0845 3010 003

English Nature
Northminster House,
Peterborough PE1 1UA.
Tel. 01733 455100;
Fax 01733 455103;
E-mail enquiries@english-
nature.org.uk; www.english-
nature.org.uk

Forest Enterprise
42 Eastgate, Pickering.
Tel. 01751 472771

National Rivers Authority
Olympia House, Gelderd Lane,
Gelderd Road, Leeds.
Tel. 0113 244 0191

National Trust
Membership and general enquiries
P0 Box 39, Bromley, Kent BR1 3XL.
Tel. 0181 315 1111;
E-mail enquires@ntrust.org.uk;
www.nationaltrust.org.uk

Regional Office
Goddards, 27 Tadcaster Road,
Dringhouses, York YO24 1GG.
Tel. 01904 702021;
Fax 01904 771970

National Park
North York Moors National Park
The Old Vicarage, Bondgate,
Helmsley YO62 5BP.
Tel. 01439 770657;
Fax 01439 770691;
E-mail general@northyorkmoors-
npa.gov.uk; www.northyorkmoors-
npa.gov.uk

Ordnance Survey
Romsey Road, Maybush,
Southampton SO16 4GU.
Tel. 08456 05 05 05 (Lo-call)
Fax: 023 8079 2615
www.ordnancesurvey.co.uk

Ramblers' Association
2nd Floor, Camelford House,
87–90 Albert Embankment,
London SE1 7TW.
Tel. 020 7339 8500

Across the fields to Helmsley Castle

Youth Hostels Association
Trevelyan House,
Dimple Road, Matlock
Debyshire DE4 3YH
Tel. 01629 592600

Local organisations

**Ryedale Folk Museum and
National Park Information Point**
Hutton-le-Hole YO6 6UA.
Tel. 01751 417367

Forest Enterprise
Low Dalby, Pickering YO17 7LT.
Tel. 01751 460295

North Yorkshire Moors Railway
Pickering Station
Tel. 01751 472508

The Old Coastguard Station
Robin Hood's Bay.
Tel. 01947 885900

Yorkshire Wildlife Trust
10 Toft Green, York.
Tel. 01904 659570

**Yorkshire and Humberside
Tourist Board**
312 Tadcaster Road, York.
Tel. 01904 707961

Visitor Centres

South Cleveland Heritage Centre
Margrove Park, Guisborough
TS12 3BZ.
Tel. 01287 610368

**Guisborough Forest and Walkway
Visitor Centre**
Pinchinthorpe Station,
Guisborough TS14 8HD.
Tel. 01287 631132

National Trust Coastal Centre
Ravenscar, Scarborough.
Tel. 01723 870138/870423

Sutton Bank National Park Centre
Sutton Bank, Thirsk YO7 2EH.
Tel. 01845 597426;
E-mail Suttonbank@ytbtic.co.uk

The Moors Centre
Danby, Whitby YO21 2NB.
Tel. 01287 660654;

Fax 01287 660308;
E-mail moorscentre@ytbtic.co.uk

Local Tourist Information Centres

Great Ayton: 01642 722835
Guisborough: 01287 633801
Helmsley: 01439 771881
Pickering: 01751 473791
Saltburn: 01287 622422
Scarborough: 01723 373333
Thirsk: 01845 522755
Whitby: 01947 602674

Public Transport

Bus Traveline
0870 608 2 608
National Rail Enquires
08457 48 49 50
(www.thetrainline.com)

Ordnance Survey Maps

Explorer OL26
(North York Moors - Western)
Explorer OL27
(North York Moors - Eastern)

Answers to Questions

Walk 1: The crow, a large, black bird, not dissimilar to a rook. It is sometimes said that if you see a rook on its own, it is probably a crow, but a flock of crows are more likely to be rooks.

Walk 2: Look above its doorway for the date – 1790.

Walk 3: It can be found among the Low Bridestones on the eastern side of Bridestone Griff.

Walk 4: They assisted ladies and the less-nimble in remounting their horses after attending service.

Walk 5: An acorn, which is depicted in the monument at the end of the walk.

Walk 6: 1857 – you will find the date on a stone plaque by the bottom of the steps at the start of the walk. In fact, the coating of limewash was finally completed on 4 November.

Walk 7: The symbols for 11 of Britain's National Parks, including the one for this park, Young Ralph's Cross.

Walk 8: A fox. The stone is actually a gravemarker, carved for Bobbie Dowson, who served as whip to the hounds of the Bilsdale Hunt.

Walk 9: An inscription on the monument relates that he was killed at Owhyhee on February 14th 1799.

Walk 10: St Peter, the patron saint of fishermen.

Walk 11: An information panel explains how coastguards trained here, firing rescue rockets at a post erected to simulate a ship's mast.

Walk 12: Crayfish – look on the information panel by the car park to discover what else to look out for.

Walk 13: £20 – you will find a board at the back of the church listing the donations.

Walk 14: A well to St Cedd is on the right as you walk to the church and another to St Chad lies on the right as you climb out of the village towards the moor.

Walk 15: On the west screen and lectern. They are the trademark of the Robert Thompson workshop at Kilburn.

Walk 16: 13th-century tiles, decorated with geometric patterns in yellow and green. Some survive in the abbey and more are displayed in the small museum there.

Walk 17: A pick-wielding quarryman standing beside a barrow containing alum shale rubble.

Walk 18: A nearby stone tablet indicates it was probably dug by 13th-century monks from Malton Priory, as a watering hole for their grazing livestock.

Walk 19: The sign behind Lowther House informs you that it is part of the Duchy of Lancaster Estates; in other words, it belongs to the Queen.

Walk 20: A notice by the car park tells you it is £5. Of course, you should not pick any wild flowers, but leave them for others to enjoy and allow them to re-seed for the following year.